Medieval World

Science and Technology
in the Middle Ages

Joanne Findon and Marsha Groves

Crabtree Publishing Company

www.crabtreebooks.com

Crabtree Publishing Company

www.crabtreebooks.com

Coordinating editor: Ellen Rodger

Project editor: Carrie Gleason

Designer and production coordinator: Rosie Gowsell

Production assistant: Samara Parent

Scanning technician: Arlene Arch-Wilson

Art director: Rob MacGregor

Project development, editing, photo editing, and layout:
First Folio Resource Group, Inc.: Tom Dart, Debbie Smith,
Anikó Szocs

Proofreading: Lynne Elliott

Photo research: Maria DeCambra

Consultant: Isabelle Cochelin, University of Toronto

Photographs: Archivo Iconografico, S.A./Corbis/Magma: p. 14
(bottom); Art Archive/Album/Joseph Martin: p. 20 (top right);
Art Archive/Bodleian Library Oxford/Bodley Or 133 folio 29r:
p. 22 (top right); Art Archive/British Library: cover; Art Archive/
Musée Condé Chantilly/Dagli Orti: p. 27 (bottom); Art Archive/
National Museum Damascus Syria/Dagli Orti: p. 28 (top right);
Art Archive/University Library Prague/Dagli Orti: p. 15 (bottom
right); Bibliothèque Nationale, Paris, France/Archives Charmet/
Bridgeman Art Library: p. 26; Bibliothèque Municipale, Rouen,
France, Lauros/Giraudon/Bridgeman Art Library: p. 11 (top left);
British Library/Add. 28681 f.9: p. 31 (bottom right); British
Library/Add. 42130 f.170: p. 7 (top); British Library/HIP/The
Image Works: p. 6 (top right), p. 11 (bottom right), p. 23 (top
right), p. 27 (top); British Library/Royal 15 E. III f.269: p. 12 (top
right); British Library/Topham-HIP/The Image Works: p. 20
(bottom left); British Museum/HIP/The Image Works: p. 31 (top
left); British Museum/Topham-HIP/The Image Works: p. 25
(bottom left); Fitzwilliam Museum, University of Cambridge,
UK/Bridgeman Art Library: p. 24; Owen Franken/
Corbis/Magma: p. 28 (bottom left); Granger Collection, New
York: p. 13 (top right), p. 16, p. 17 (top right), p. 18 (bottom), p. 19,
p. 29 (bottom right); Angelo Hornak/Corbis/Magma: p. 17
(bottom left); Kremlin Museums, Moscow, Russia/Bridgeman Art
Library: p. 18 (top); New York Public Library/Art Resource, NY:
p. 10 (bottom left); The Pierpont Morgan Library/Art Resource,
NY: p. 30; Scala/Art Resource, NY: p. 5 (bottom right), p. 10 (top
right), p. 13 (bottom left), p. 23 (bottom left); Snark/Art Resource,
NY: title page

Map: Samara Parent, Margaret Amy Reiach

Illustrations: Jeff Crosby: pp. 8–9, p. 14 (top); Connie Gleason: p.5
(map icons), p. 12 (bottom), p. 15 (top), p. 21, p. 22 (bottom), p. 29
(top); Katherine Kantor: flags, title page (border), copyright page
(bottom); Margaret Amy Reiach: borders, gold boxes, title page
(illuminated letter), copyright page (top), contents page
(background), pp. 4-5 (timeline), p. 6 (bottom), p. 7 (bottom),
p. 32 (all)

Cover: During the Middle Ages, people invented new
technologies and ways of doing work that made tasks such as
constructing stone buildings much easier.

Title page: In the Middle Ages, astronomers used devices called
astrolabes to measure the movement of the stars.

Crabtree Publishing Company

www.crabtreebooks.com   1-800-387-7650

Cataloging-in-Publication Data
Findon, Joanne.
Science and technology in the Middle Ages / written by
Joanne Findon and Marcia Groves.
p. cm. -- (The medieval world)
Includes index.
ISBN 0-7787-1354-7 (RLB) -- ISBN 0-7787-1386-5 (pbk)
1. Science, Medieval--Juvenile literature. 2. Technology--
History--To 1500--Juvenile literature. I. Groves, Marcia.
II. Title. III. Medieval worlds series.
Q124.97.G76 2005
509.4'09'02--dc22
                                        2004013062
                                              LC

Published in
the United States
PMB 16A
350 Fifth Ave.
Suite 3308
New York, NY
10118

Published
in Canada
616 Welland Ave.,
St. Catharines,
Ontario, Canada
L2M 5V6

Published in the
United Kingdom
73 Lime Walk
Headington
Oxford
0X3 7AD
United Kingdom

Published
in Australia
386 Mt. Alexander Rd.,
Ascot Vale (Melbourne)
V1C 3032

Table of Contents

Ideas and Inventions

From about 100 B.C. to 500 A.D., the area from England to the Middle East **was under** Roman **control. The Romans built long roads, large cities, and deep mines throughout their** empire. **Hundreds, sometimes thousands, of people worked on these difficult projects.**

The Roman Empire began to break up around 400 A.D. There was no longer one central government to plan large projects and keep law and order. Roads crumbled and travel became more dangerous. It was difficult for people to journey to trade goods, such as cloth and food, and to share ideas and inventions.

The Middle Ages

The Middle Ages, or medieval period, began around 500 A.D. and ended around 1500 A.D. in western Europe. During the Middle Ages, small to large kingdoms were established. Kings, nobles, and Church leaders ruled the land, but most people were peasants, who farmed their own small strips of land and the land of their **lords**. Others were traders, craftspeople, knights, **monks**, and **nuns**.

▼ *Kings and important nobles gave parcels of land, called manors, to their most loyal supporters. In exchange, they were given knights, or warriors on horseback, to fight for them in times of war. Peasants made up the majority of the population, but they had the least power.*

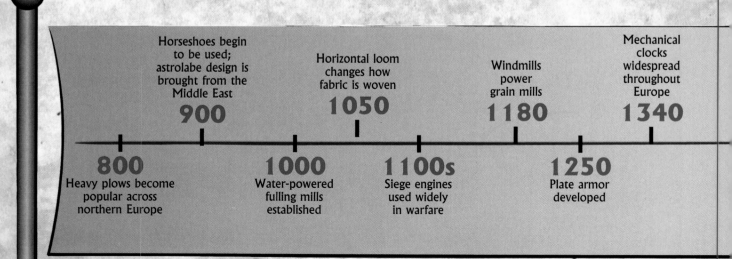

Horseshoes begin to be used; astrolabe design is brought from the Middle East
900

Horizontal loom changes how fabric is woven
1050

Windmills power grain mills
1180

Mechanical clocks widespread throughout Europe
1340

800
Heavy plows become popular across northern Europe

1000
Water-powered fulling mills established

1100s
Siege engines used widely in warfare

1250
Plate armor developed

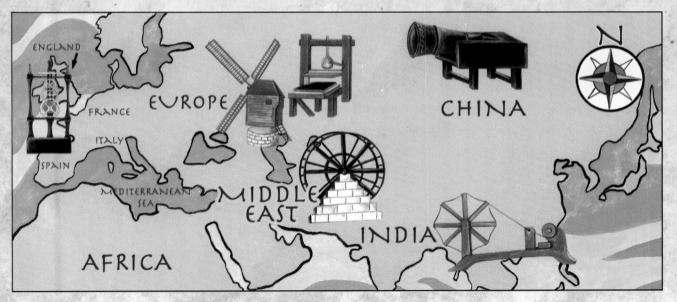

▲ *Many medieval inventions and scientific discoveries came from Europe; others were brought from places such as China, India, and the Middle East.*

Making Work Easier

New ways of farming developed during the Middle Ages that allowed fewer peasants to produce more food, so more people could live in towns and cities. By 1200 A.D., trade to distant places was becoming common, and ideas from the Middle East and Asia reached Europe.

Some jobs that were done by hand at the beginning of the Middle Ages were done with the help of machines in the later Middle Ages. New technology made work and travel quicker and easier.

Cannon perfected; gunpowder improved; printing press developed in Germany

1450

1380
Blast furnace makes cast iron possible

▲ *In the Middle Ages, barrels were used for storing food, bathing, washing and dyeing cloth, and holding ale and wine. The cooper, or barrelmaker, made water-tight barrels from carefully shaped strips of oak, called staves. The staves were held together snugly with circles of iron, copper, or bent wood.*

Farming

Peasants in the Middle Ages lived in small villages. The villages were surrounded by fields where the peasants grew food for most of the population.

Three-Field Rotation

In the early Middle Ages, peasants planted a field one year and let it lie fallow, or unplanted, the next so the soil could regain its **nutrients**. Only half the fields were planted with crops each year.

In the late 700s, farmers began using a three-field rotation for planting. Fields were divided into three groups, instead of two. The first group of fields was planted with wheat or rye in autumn. The second was planted in spring with oats, beans, peas, lentils, or vegetables. The third was left fallow. This way, peasants grew crops in two-thirds of the fields each year, rather than in only half.

▲ *Medieval peasants used scythes to cut hay at harvest time. The cut hay was raked into piles and loaded onto a cart to be taken back to the barn for winter storage.*

◀ *Farming was done by hand with tools peasants made for themselves or with the help of the village blacksmith. Sickles were used to cut wheat.*

The Heavy Plow

Around 800 A.D., new iron-bladed plows were invented to prepare the heavy, damp soil of northern Europe for planting. Known as heavy plows, they had wooden frames and three iron attachments called plow-irons. Two plow-irons were cutting blades that sliced strips of **turf** off the fields. The third piece, the moldboard, tipped the turf over to form a neat ridge. Seeds were scattered in the furrows, which are the spaces between the ridges, and on the sloping sides of the ridges.

▲ *The heavy plow prepared the fields for planting by digging deep into the soil.*

Horse Power

The heavy plow required a team of oxen or horses to pull it. Oxen were strong, but very slow. Horses moved faster and could do much more work if they had the right harnesses, sturdy horseshoes, and enough oats to eat.

In the 700s, a new way of harnessing horses reached Europe from Asia. Instead of using a leather strap that went around the horse's neck, a padded leather U-shaped collar rested on the horse's shoulders. With this new harness, horses could pull heavy loads without choking.

▲ *Iron horseshoes first appeared in the late 800s, and by 1050 all working horses wore shoes. They protected horses' sensitive hoofs from damp, rough ground.*

The Mill

For thousands of years, people have turned the energy of flowing water into power to do work. Water power was used wherever possible in medieval Europe to do work more quickly and efficiently than with human power alone.

The turning motion of waterwheels built by rushing streams, on barges, and by ocean tides, powered gristmills, which ground grain into flour. By 1000 A.D., medieval craftspeople also used waterwheels to power up-and-down motions, such as raising and lowering hammers, pumping **bellows**, and pounding cloth.

By 1180, people in Europe were also using wind power to do work. They built windmills, which had sails that caught the energy from the wind to turn **axles** and gears. Windmills were very popular in northern Europe, where water froze in winter and waterwheels could not turn.

The water is released in a narrow mill–race to increase its force.

The dam holds water.

Grain is poured
into the hopper.

The top millstone
turns slowly and grinds
the grain into flour.

This axle turns more
slowly. It is connected
to the top millstone.

The gears turn
and mesh with
other gears.

The axle
attached to the
wheel turns
very quickly.

A wheel with
paddles or
buckets captures
the moving
water and spins.

Making Cloth

In the Middle Ages, cloth making employed more people than any other trade except farming. Textiles were needed not only for clothing, but also for many other uses, such as sacks and food wrapping. Cloth was most often made from sheep's wool or from linen. Linen is made from a plant called flax. The finest cloth was made of silk, which comes from silkworms.

▲ *Sheep were sheared in early summer.*

Preparing Wool

Wool was cut from sheep using heavy metal scissors called shears. After the fleece was washed, it was combed with carding combs, which were flat, wooden paddles covered with sharp metal pins. Carding made wool straight and smooth.

Preparing Flax

The flax plant grew all over Europe. Its woody stems contain fine fibers that are used to make cloth and rope. After flax plants were harvested, their stems were soaked in water until they began to fall apart. The soaked stems were pounded with wooden tools called scutches until the fine fibers separated from the woody parts. Then, the flax was washed, combed, and spun into linen thread.

◀ *A carder placed a tuft of clean wool between two combs and stroked the combs together until the wool was untangled.*

▲ *All women, whether noble or peasant, spent many hours each day making thread to be woven into cloth for their household.*

Spinning

Thread and yarn were made by hand. A tuft of combed wool or linen was wound around a long rod, called a distaff. The loose end of the tuft was attached to a short, thin stick, called a spindle. From the bottom of the spindle hung a small, round weight called a spindle whorl. The spindle and whorl were twirled so they spun like a top. The movement twisted the wool or linen fibers into a tight thread.

In the late 1200s, the spinning wheel, which had been widely used in India, became known in medieval Europe. Spinning wheels helped spinsters make thread more quickly, but the thread was loose and rough. The distaff and spindle were still used to make the tight, smooth threads needed for fine cloth.

▼ *The spinning wheel's large upright wheel was turned by hand or by crank. The turning wheel moved a belt. The belt moved a very small wheel, which turned the spindle.*

Guilds

Many medieval craftspeople organized guilds, which were groups of people who worked in a single craft. Guilds agreed on rules and regulations for making and selling their products, trained new craftspeople, and shared trade secrets among members. Cloth making had many guilds, including guilds for weavers, dyers, and **embroiderers**.

Dyeing

After thread was spun, it was soaked in a vat of water and dye. Most dyes were made from plants. Buckthorn berries made a yellow dye, madder root, a red dye, and woad plants, a blue dye. Some colors, such as green, were difficult to make. Dyes were combined with ingredients called mordants to help fibers hold color or make colors brighter. Some common mordants were the chemical alum, metals such as copper and iron, and tannin, from oak bark and twigs. Cloth makers kept dye recipes secret because each wanted to have the best, most permanent colors.

▲ *Cloth could also be dyed after it was woven.*

Weaving

Cloth was woven on a long, rectangular wooden frame called a loom. Sturdy threads, called the warp, were fastened lengthwise along the loom. The weaver wrapped another thread, called the weft, around a flat holder, called the shuttle. The weft was woven through the warp, passing below one warp thread and above the next one. Once the shuttle reached the far side of the loom, it was turned and the weft thread was woven back to the other side. Until the 1000s, most looms were upright and weavers worked standing up. After 1050, weavers sat at horizontal looms set on table-height frames.

Looms became more like machines in the later Middle Ages. By 1250, looms had foot pedals attached to bars through which the warp was threaded. When the weaver pressed a pedal, the bar lifted a group of threads so that the weaver could pass the shuttle under them. The weaver then let the raised threads drop and lifted up new threads.

woven cloth

shuttle

warp

bobbin with weft thread

foot pedals

◀ *A weaver worked very quickly on a horizontal loom, thumping on the foot pedals and using both hands to guide the shuttle back and forth.*

Fulling

Cloth was loosely woven when it came off the loom. A process called fulling made it tight, smooth, and durable. Woven cloth was bundled up and placed in a trough or tub. The tub was filled with water and a soapy clay called fuller's earth, urine, or a chemical called potash. The cloth was pounded and turned until all its fibers clung together tightly. Fulling also removed greasiness from wool.

In the early Middle Ages, fullers pounded cloth by stepping on it. In England, people who did this job were called walkers. The finest woolen cloth was always fulled by foot, but from 1050 on, more and more pounding was done by machine at fulling mills. These mills used water power to raise and lower mallets or hammers that thumped down onto the soaking cloth.

Tanning

In the Middle Ages, leather was used to make shoes, buckets, aprons, leggings, harnesses, waterproof window coverings, and book covers. Turning an animal hide into flexible, long-lasting leather was the job of the tanner. The tanner scraped fat off the skin of a slaughtered animal, then soaked the hide in a mixture of water and a chemical called lime. The mixture loosened the hair on the hide. The tanner rinsed the hide clean and scraped away the hair with a broad, flat metal blade. The hide was soaked in many changes of water, sometimes with animal manure or urine to soften the skin.

After this preparation, the hide was soaked for at least seven months in a vat filled with water and chips of oak or oak bark. Tannin, a natural chemical in oak, turns leather brown and stops it from rotting. A chemical called alum was used instead of oak when a fine, white leather was needed for fancy gloves, shoes, and books.

▲ *The tanner dried the animal hide on a frame to keep it flat.*

▲ *Fulled cloth was stretched on a wooden frame to dry. When dry, the cloth was brushed with teasels until a soft surface, or nap, formed.*

13

Building Homes

Most medieval people lived in small homes made of wood or stone. In the early Middle Ages, houses made of wood were built directly on the ground, without a stone or gravel foundation. The houses had to be rebuilt often because the damp ground rotted the wood.

By the late Middle Ages, low stone foundation walls kept wooden buildings off the wet ground. Houses still had a wooden framework, but many different materials were used to form the walls, including wattle and daub. Wattle was a screen made of woven twigs that was daubed, or coated, with mud. When the mud was dry, it was painted with a mixture of lime and water, called whitewash, which colored it white and protected it from the rain.

▲ Roofs were often thatched, or covered with bundles of straw or reeds. A thatched roof lasted more than 30 years.

◄ Sawyers cut wooden planks for houses by pulling a long saw back and forth in a sawpit.

A Carpenter's Tools

Making wooden frames was a carpenter's job. Carpenters also made wooden furniture, and made and repaired wooden tools.

◀Hammers had an iron head and were used to hammer nails

▼Chisels were used to cut notches and pegs that joined wooden beams together tightly. A plane was a chisel inside a wooden block used to smooth wood.

▲Carpenters shaped lumber with adzes.

Life at Home

Medieval homes were heated by burning wood or **peat** in a fireplace or in a small metal bowl called a brazier. The same fire was used for cooking. Food was prepared in iron pots hung above the fire and in smaller pots placed over the fire on three-legged stands called trivets. Smoke floated out of the home through holes in the roof or walls. Wood-framed homes did not have chimneys to carry the smoke away until the late 1400s.

▼*A rope and pulley were used to raise water from the well.*

Most people fetched water from a well or stream. In cities, underground pipes made of lead, clay, or hollowed-out logs brought water from country springs to public fountains, where neighbors filled their water jugs. Some city houses had private wells in their small back gardens.

Just as people needed to bring in fresh water, they needed to get rid of waste and dirty water. Some houses had privies, or outhouses. A wattle screen surrounded a wooden seat with a hole in it. More often, waste was collected in buckets and thrown into deep holes called cesspits or into gutters that drained into streams and rivers.

Built of Stone

The most important medieval structures, such as cathedrals, bridges, and castles, were made from stone. The stone was cut out of enormous pits, called quarries, with hand tools including chisels, saws, and levers. Large blocks of cut stone were lifted with hoists and loaded onto carts pulled by mules or oxen. Stone from far-away quarries was sometimes loaded on barges and floated down rivers or canals to building sites.

The Master Builder

A master builder supervised the many **masons**, carpenters, metalworkers, and laborers needed to build a large stone structure. After the master builder decided on the building's design, the outline of its walls was marked on the ground. Workers dug trenches along the lines and filled them with gravel, stone, or rubble to serve as the building's foundation.

▼ *Masons used plumb bobs, which were lead weights that hung from cords, to make sure the walls were vertical. They used levels to make sure the walls were even.*

Building Higher and Higher

Stonemasons trimmed and shaped building stones with saws, hammers, and chisels. They used measuring tools to match the stones' shape to patterns that the master builder gave them. Mortar, which was a mixture of **quicklime**, sand, and water, held the stones in place.

Scaffolding, a wooden framework with floors for workers to stand on, was attached to the building as it rose higher. Cranes, windlasses, and treadwheels lifted stones, wooden beams, iron, and lead to the higher parts of the building. A windlass raised heavy loads by using a hand-powered crank to wind rope onto a cylinder. Building supplies attached to the rope were slowly lifted up. A treadwheel, which looked like a huge hamster wheel, was sometimes built on top of the construction site to lift especially heavy materials.

▲ *Workers walked inside the treadwheel, lifting loads by slowly winding the rope onto the wheel's axle.*

Innovations in Building

Ancient and early medieval cathedrals had thick walls and rounded arches to support their high ceilings. Windows were small because builders knew that larger openings weakened walls. This architectural style is called Romanesque.

Around 1150, builders began to experiment with ways to create higher buildings full of light and space. They constructed thick stone supports, called buttresses and piers, against the outside walls. These helped the main walls carry the weight of the roof and high ceiling. The supports also made it possible to have more windows and slender, pointed arches. This architectural style is known as Gothic.

◀ *Extra supports called flying buttresses surround Bourges Cathedral in Saint Etienne, France.*

Metalworking

Metalworkers made tools, weapons, dishes, jewelry, armor, and machinery. They worked with a variety of metals, including iron, lead, copper, tin, silver, and gold.

Metals are found in a rocky mixture of minerals called ore. The ore is dug from mines deep underground.

Iron

Iron was the most important metal in medieval Europe. It was used to make hammers, nails, plow blades, axles and gears, and weapons. Every village and castle had a **forge** where a blacksmith worked.

Before metal could be used, it had to be separated from the ore. Some metals, such as copper and lead, were purified by being heated in furnaces until they melted. Until the late Middle Ages, there was no way to make iron hot enough to melt. Instead, iron ore was cleaned and crushed, then put in a furnace with a lot of charcoal.

▲ *Goldsmiths used chisels and small hammers to shape gold into beautiful pieces of jewelry. They used pointed tools to engrave complicated designs in the gold.*

▼ *Iron was used to make horseshoes, which were nailed to horses' hooves.*

Working with Iron

After the iron and charcoal were heated together, the blacksmith lifted out the glowing metal with a large pair of tongs. The smith hammered the hot iron until all the unwanted parts of the ore were forced out. Then, the remaining iron was hammered into shape. The metal was reheated as often as needed to keep it soft enough to work with.

In the 1300s, water-powered bellows made possible a new invention, the blast furnace. A blast furnace uses extra oxygen to make a fire hot enough to melt iron. The liquid iron was cast, or poured into molds, to make hundreds of identical objects, such as cannonballs.

Working with Steel

With practice, medieval blacksmiths learned to make steel, which is iron combined with a tiny amount of **carbon**. Steel is very strong and flexible. Armorers used it to make weapons and suits of armor to protect knights.

In the early Middle Ages, armor was made of small iron rings linked together, called chain mail. Beginning in 1250, armorers began to use flat pieces of iron or steel connected with rivets and leather straps to form suits of armor. By 1450, knights were covered from head to toe with steel plates.

▼ *Hot iron was hammered on a stand, called an anvil, to be shaped into pieces of armor.*

Weapons

Medieval swords were made of iron and, later, steel. Knights fought with long, heavy swords that needed two hands to lift, and with shorter, thinner swords that slipped through the gaps between a suit of armor's metal plates.

Bows and Arrows

Bows and arrows were used to attack distant soldiers and horses on the battlefield and to defend castle walls. New styles of bows were invented in the Middle Ages that could shoot farther and with greater force than earlier bows.

Archers from **Wales** and England were famous for using longbows, which were as tall as the bowmen firing them. Longbows took great skill to aim and strength to pull. Good archers could fire a dozen arrows in a minute. Longbows became the most dangerous battlefield weapon.

▲ *Most swords were useful for both thrusting and slashing. They had a sharp point that pierced through the gaps between plates of armor and at least one cutting edge to cut off an enemy's arms, legs, or head.*

A crossbow was a small, T-shaped bow. To fire, the crossbow was held flat, and its string was pulled back with a small crank. When the trigger was pulled, a small, metal-tipped arrow called a bolt flew more than 250 yards (230 meters) with so much power it could pierce armor.

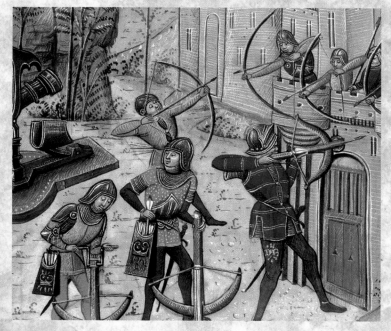

◄ *Armies used both longbows and crossbows when laying siege to an enemy's castle. Crossbows were easy to shoot, but difficult to load. They could fire only one or two bolts each minute.*

Siege Engines

To take an enemy's castle, armies surrounded, or besieged, the castle and waited for its defenders to run out of food, firewood, and arrows. Meanwhile, soldiers tried to break through the castle walls using machines called siege engines. Some siege engines, such as mangonels, used the power from unwinding tightly twisted ropes to throw rocks and other **ammunition** at castle walls.

▼ Trebuchets, which were about 30 feet (nine meters) tall, had wheels so they could be moved around a castle's walls.

The trebuchet was a huge siege engine developed in the Middle Ages. Trebuchets looked like giant seesaws, with one short side and one long side. The long side was the flinging arm, with a sling at the end to hold a large rock or other ammunition. The short side had a heavy weight attached to it. Soldiers pulled down the long side with ropes, held it in place with a locking pin, and loaded the ammunition into the sling. When the locking pin was pulled out, the heavy, shorter side lowered suddenly and flung the long arm upward, throwing the ammunition into the castle wall.

Gunpowder

In the 1200s, warriors returning from the Middle East introduced gunpowder to Europe. At first, gunpowder, which was a Chinese invention, exploded unpredictably, injuring the soldiers who used it. By the 1400s, gunpowder had been improved, and more soldiers were fighting with cannon and small guns. Castle walls could not withstand these weapons, and soon castles were no longer places of safety.

Alchemy

Medieval alchemists were the first European chemists, or scientists who mix chemicals. They read books by ancient philosophers and scientists, and conducted experiments to try to understand the substances that made up the world around them.

Many alchemists' ideas came from Arabic language books introduced to Europe in the 1200s. These books explained what metals are made of, how to combine metals, and how to change one metal into another. Other ideas came from ancient Chinese, Greek, and Egyptian magic. An alchemist from China named Ge Hong (281 A.D. to 361 A.D.) wrote down his observations about magnets and about poisons and their cures. He also searched for a potion, called the elixir of life, that would bring people good health and keep them young forever.

▲ *Medieval alchemists studied Arabic books on alchemy that were brought to Europe after 1200.*

The Elixir of Life

Many European alchemists also searched for the elixir of life. They tried to make the elixir by heating and **distilling** liquids, such as alcohol, to purify them. Alchemists had many recipes for creating the elixir, but they did their best to keep the details secret so that only trained alchemists would be able to make them. In the end, no recipe was successful.

◀ *An alchemist used an apparatus such as this one to distill liquids.*

Making Gold

By the 1300s, many European alchemists were searching for ways to make gold out of common metals. They learned a lot about metals, but no alchemist was able to make gold, although some tricked people by making substances that looked and felt like gold.

▶ *Alchemists melted metals in hot furnaces and mixed them with other melted metals or with substances such as herbs, hair, blood, and animal dung to try to make gold.*

Albertus Magnus and Roger Bacon

Albertus Magnus and Roger Bacon became known as the most important alchemists of the Middle Ages. Rather than relying solely on old books, Albertus Magnus visited mines to observe the heating and cooling of metals. Roger Bacon did chemical experiments in his own laboratory, writing down in clear language the details of what he did.

◀ *Albertus Magnus was the first scientist of medieval Europe to develop and record chemical experiments.*

Making Books

Books were rare and valuable during the Middle Ages. Making a book required a tanner to prepare the pages, an apothecary to provide the pigments for ink, and a scribe to copy the text. Books took months or even years to produce.

Parchment, Vellum, and Paper

In medieval Europe, most books were written on parchment, which is prepared from the skin of calves. Very special books used vellum, a finer hide made from young lambs. When the parchment or vellum had been tanned and dried, it was polished with a light, spongy stone called pumice. Then, it was pressed flat and rubbed with chalk until it was smooth and pale enough to write on.

The first paper was made in China before 100 A.D., but paper did not become well known in western Europe until the 1200s. To make paper, workers in Europe shredded and soaked scraps of cloth, then pounded the mixture in water-powered pulping machines until it looked like a messy soup. The soupy mixture, called pulp, was spread over fine screens, drained, and pressed until it formed a dry sheet. Like parchment, paper had to be made smooth and cut to the right size before it was a good writing surface.

▲ *The most beautiful manuscripts had pictures called illuminations that seemed to illuminate, or light up, the page. Some illuminations were decorated with finely hammered sheets of gold called gold leaf.*

A Scribe's Work

To keep the writing straight, a scribe marked straight lines on a blank page with a piece of soft lead or a pointed metal stick called a stylus. The scribe wrote with a quill pen made by sharpening a point at the end of a hollow goose feather. A small knife was used to trim the quill whenever it bent or frayed. The scribe dipped the quill in ink. Some ink was made by mixing a fine black soot, called lampblack, with sticky tree gum. Other inks, called iron-gall inks, were made from plant materials containing a type of acid called tannic acid.

▶ *Until nearly the end of the Middle Ages, all books were hand-written by scribes. Scribes were educated people, mostly monks and nuns, who could read and write.*

▲ *By 1455, printers were using movable type to produce official documents, religious books such as the Bible, and law texts.*

The Printing Press

In the early 1400s, inventors in Germany began to experiment with ways of printing books by machine, rather than copying them by hand. They hoped that printing would speed up book production and make books less expensive to buy.

A German printer, named Johannes Gutenberg, devised a printing method called movable type. It was similar to a system already used in China. The type was made up of individual blocks of wood or lead into which letters and punctuation marks were cut. A printer arranged the type to spell the words on each page. The letters were coated in ink, and paper was pressed firmly down onto the type using a machine called a screw-press. The type was then moved around to arrange new pages.

Medicine

People living in medieval cities hired doctors, surgeons, and apothecaries to take care of them when they were sick.

Medieval doctors knew what the human body looked like inside, but they did not fully understand how it worked. Some had studied at a medical school that was started in Italy in the 1100s. Doctors who trained there learned about the human body from Greek, Roman, and Arabic medical books that had not been well known in Europe before. Unfortunately, many of the treatments described in these books did not cure diseases. Doctors did not know that germs caused illnesses, because microscopes, which are needed to see germs, were not invented until 1674.

The Humors

Many people in the Middle Ages believed that some sicknesses were punishments sent by God or were caused by the movement of planets. They believed that other illnesses were caused by a lack of balance in the body among four liquids called humors. The four humors were yellow bile, black bile, blood, and **phlegm**. Sickness came when there was too much or too little of each humor. Doctors often suggested that patients eat or drink mixtures of herbs to restore the balance among the humors.

If the problem was too much of one humor, purges, which were medicines made from herbs, were used to get rid of some of the humor. If a patient had too much blood, a doctor would "let," or release, blood from the person's body.

▲ *Apothecaries mixed and made drugs using herbs, spices, and minerals.*

▲ *Patients lined up to visit doctors and surgeons. Their urine was inspected to diagnose illnesses. If bloodletting was required, surgeons released blood by making a cut in a vein, or they used slug-like creatures called leeches to suck out the blood.*

Herbal Remedies

People in the Middle Ages treated less serious illnesses with medicines made from plants and herbs. Fennel seeds were used to cure stomach problems. Cloths soaked in the boiled roots of the comfrey plant were wrapped around broken bones to help them mend more quickly. Yarrow leaves were applied to cuts and wounds to stop bleeding, and a tea made with yarrow was used to ease toothaches.

Surgery

Barbers in the Middle Ages were often surgeons as well. They removed rotten teeth, set broken bones, and stitched up wounds that would not stop bleeding. Rags dipped in mixtures of strong herbs, such as henbane, opium, and the mandrake root, were held to patients' nostrils to lessen the pain. Infections after surgery were common, and many patients died.

▶ *By the 1300s, some surgeons used trepanning to relieve severe headaches and to treat mental illness. Trepanning involved cutting open the skull to relieve pressure from swelling or, as some believed, to release evil spirits.*

Astronomy and Timekeeping

In the Middle Ages, people used the moon, sun, and stars to tell time and to navigate, or determine their location, at sea. Medieval astrologers, astronomers, **and navigators developed special instruments to help them keep track of the movements of the sun and stars.**

The Astrolabe

Astrolabes were instruments made of several movable brass disks that could be adjusted to make a map of the sky. The edge of the bottom disk was marked with the degrees of a circle and the hours of the day. The upper disks had marks showing the position of the stars and the sun. By lining up the astrolabe's markings with the **horizon** and objects in the sky, people could tell the hour and the month.

▲ *Astrolabes were introduced to Europe from the Middle East in the 900s.*

Clocks

Most people in the Middle Ages were peasants who relied on the sun to tell time and never needed a clock. The first people to keep track of the hours were monks and nuns who prayed at certain times of day. As city life grew, other people needed to know what time it was so they could run their businesses and follow city rules, such as **curfew**. At first, clocks did not have hour hands, just loud bells that rang out the hours and quarter hours.

◀ *Most medieval clocks were built on the towers of churches and city halls so that they were easy to see and hear.*

Water and Mechanical Clocks

Some early medieval clocks used water to measure time. One type was a water clock, which steadily dripped a measured amount of water into a cylinder marked with the hours of the day. As long as the water dripped at the right rate, people could tell the hour by looking at the mark the water had reached.

By 1330, most clocks were powered by a weight attached to a cord. The cord was wrapped around an axle. As the weight dropped, the axle turned. This motion turned many interlocking gears that moved the clock's hands and struck its bells. This type of clock is called a mechanical clock. By 1370, small mechanical clocks were built for homes and businesses.

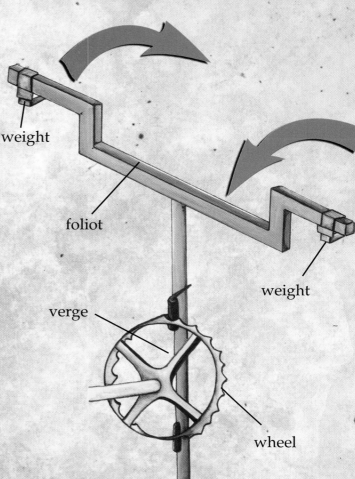

weight

foliot

verge

weight

wheel

▶ *A medieval invention called a verge-and-foliot escapement helped clock gears keep steady time. The foliot, or bar across the top, swings back and forth. The weights on either side hits and turns the wheel, causing it to turn.*

An Astronomical Clock

A famous clock was built in China between 1086 A.D. and 1094 A.D. It was powered by collecting water in a series of tipping buckets designed to keep steady time. Its machinery, or clockwork, filled a 40 foot (12 meter) tower and showed the movements of the sun, moon, and stars as well as the hours and quarter hours. Within one hundred years, all that was left of the clock was a description in a book.

▶ *No other clocks like this Chinese astronomical clock were ever built.*

Transportation

During the Middle Ages, most people traveled on foot, although travelers sometimes rode on horses, mules, or carts. Thousands of miles of well-paved roads had been built during the time of the Roman Empire, but by 400 A.D., they were no longer maintained. In their place, and in areas where roads had never been built, there were rough, muddy tracks along which travelers struggled.

Wagons

Horse-drawn wagons were used to haul heavy loads. The design of wagons improved during the Middle Ages. By the early 1100s, sturdy four-wheeled wagons were common, instead of smaller two-wheeled carts. The new wagons had strong iron axles that pivoted when the horses turned, so even long wagons could be steered smoothly. Hand brakes were developed to slow and stop the wagons.

▼ *At first, horses' harnesses were attached to fixed poles, and the poles were connected to wagons. These were replaced by harnesses attached to swinging poles called singletrees. Singletrees made it easier for drivers, such as these soldiers, to steer and for horses to turn.*

Travel on Water

Whenever possible, people and goods traveled by water. Travel by water was quicker and easier than by land since there were no difficult roads to slow the journey. Medieval boats were made of wood. Some boats were rowed, but most ships that went on long voyages of trade or exploration were powered by wind trapped in large square sails.

Tools invented or improved during the Middle Ages, such as the quadrant and compass, made it possible to navigate on the open sea. Sailors also used a type of astrolabe to estimate their location at sea by checking the positions of the sun or stars.

▲ *The mariner's quadrant showed the altitude, or height, of the North Star above the horizon. By checking where the North Star was, it was possible to figure out how far north the ship lay.*

Maps

Beginning around 800 A.D., mapmakers in the Middle East made maps based on the idea that the earth was a sphere. **Latitude** and **longitude** were used to locate places on a map. These ideas were not used in Europe until 1375 A.D.

By 1050, the *mappa mundi*, or map of the world, was the most common map in western Europe. This map was circular and showed Europe and those parts of Asia and Africa that Europeans knew at the time.

Using new navigational guides, medieval explorers were able to travel further from home, visit new lands, and return with information about the world beyond Europe. The maps they made changed to show countries they had not known about before.

▲ *Mapmakers placed the Middle Eastern city of Jerusalem in the center of the mappa mundi. Jerusalem was both the birthplace of the Christian religion and a symbol of the perfect city.*

Glossary

ammunition Objects, such as rocks, bullets, or cannonballs, fired during an attack

apothecary A person who makes and sells medicines and herbs

astrologer A person who studies how the stars, moon, and planets affect events on Earth and human behavior

astronomer A person who studies the moon, stars, and planets

axle A pole on which a wheel turns

barge A flat-bottomed boat used to transport goods

bellows A device used to pump air

canal A man-made waterway

carbon A non-metallic material found in nature

cathedral The main church in an area led by a bishop

curfew An order that requires people to be off the streets at a certain time

distill To heat a liquid or solid until it sends off steam, then to gather and cool the steam until it becomes liquid again. This process is used to purify a substance

embroiderer A person who decorates fabric with designs made by needlework

empire A group of countries or territories under one ruler or government

forge An oven or workshop with an oven where metal is heated and hammered into shape

foundation The base or support on which something is built

horizon The line where the land or sea meets the sky

latitude The distance north or south of the equator

longitude The distance east or west from the prime meridian, an imaginary line that passes through Greenwich, England

lord A powerful person who rules people on his land

mason A person who builds with stone or brick

Middle East The region made up of southwestern Asia and northern Africa

monk A male member of a religious community who devotes his life to prayer and study

nun A female member of a religious community who devotes her life to prayer and study

nutrient A substance living things need for growth

peat Very rich soil made of decaying plants, used as fuel or fertilizer

philosopher A person who studies truth, right and wrong, God, and the meaning of life

phlegm A thick, sticky substance made in the nose and throat to moisten and protect them

pigment A colored powder or liquid made from plants and animals, used as coloring

quicklime A dry, white material used to make mortar and plaster

Roman Relating to the Roman empire. The Roman empire was a group of territories under the control of Rome

siege The act of surrounding a city or fortress in order to capture it

teasel The head of a prickly flower, used to comb cloth in order to raise its surface

textile Cloth

turf The top layer of soil, with grass and its roots

Wales The western part of the island of Great Britain

Index

1 2 3 4 5 6 7 8 9 0   Printed in the U.S.A.   1 0 9 8 7 6 5

2   4/07